She Is Beauty

Redefining Beauty In The 21st Century

Table Of Contents

1. "I wish I looked like her."

2. "You should look like this."

3. "You're too..."

4. "I'm so ugly."

5. "You're so full of yourself."

6. "That's way too high."

7. "Will you be my girlfriend?"

8. "New diet starts today."

9. "I'm not hungry."

10.   "You look pretty today."

11.   "Girl, you're stunning."

12.   "She's cute, but..."

13.   "I think I'm in love."

14.   "You're beautiful."

15.   "No junk food."

16.   "She's so kind."

17.   "Just the way you are."

18.   The Author's Note.

There is a blank page after each chapter just in case you want to take notes

For My Mom,

Thank you for showing me how to let my inward

beauty shine and appreciate my outward beauty.

Love you always.

Introduction:

Girl, I get it. Life is TOUGH. We have tons of things we have to deal with. One of them in particular is body issues. That's why I wrote this.

Hi. I'm Reese. I'm a 15-year-old girl who knows all about the struggles. I'm here to tell you what the LORD says, why society doesn't get to determine your value, and how to really, truly love who you are. I'll also talk to you about the horrible things we have to deal with *because* we're girls. I've struggled with all of these things at least once in my life, and I have friends who struggle with them daily.

All of this started with an Instagram post. On Easter of 2020, I posted 3 pictures: one of my acne, one of my stomach, and one of my side profile. Guess what those are? Don't worry, I'll tell you.

Those right there are my biggest insecurities, and I posted them for everyone to see. I initially did it for me. I wanted to allow myself to show other people that I should recognize these skin-deep insecurities as the things that make me beautiful and unique, not the things that should make me ashamed of or discouraged with the way I look. Then, after the post had been up for a while, I started getting a lot of positive feedback. This made me realize that I'm definitely not the only girl out there struggling.

Flash forward to July, and I made another post about it, only this time, I touched on the topic of confidence vs. insecurities. Again, I got a ton of positive feedback. I noticed these kinds of posts do not tend to get as many "likes" or "hits" as my others. I've even had people unfollow me, but I'm okay with that because what's important to me is I helped girls feel more comfortable in their own skin. To me, that's worth a million likes. I even saw a girl post a selfie and tag me in it with the caption: "Thanks for the confidence boost!". That's why I do this. That's why I invest so much time into writing and conversing with girls.

Being a girl is hard, but, hopefully, this will make you see just how amazing you really are. Do you want to feel comfortable in your own skin? Let me show you how and why you should. Let's learn to love ourselves...one chapter at a time.

chapter 1

"I wish I looked like her."

Comparison. It's a hefty topic because it's something we all struggle with, but I've noticed it's not talked about. Comparison is like cancer. It gradually tears you apart. I used to have this "comparison cancer" a while ago. I healed. This is the treatment that helped me abolish it.

Let me take a moment to tell you about my stunning best friend. She's got curly blonde hair, freckles, clear skin, and a great body figure. She looks like one of those beachy girls that wake up and go surfing every morning. She eats healthy and goes on runs, so she's slim. Let me tell you something else: I wanted all of those things.

Being my best friend means we spend a lot of time together. I have to look at everything she has that I don't almost every day. That used to eat me up inside. I would sit there and stare at her, hoping, longing, *wishing* for the things she had. That's when I realized something. Those are the things that make her unique. Those are the things that make her beauty different from my beauty. Our differences are what make up our beauty.

She once told me she wishes she had my eyes. So you see, there are things about me that she admires. Now, I'm not saying that her wishing for something I have is good, just like me wishing for something she has isn't either. I'm saying that we all have things that other people think are unique and beautiful about us.

Someone once told me that butterflies can't see the color of their wings, so they have no clue of how beautiful they are. You only see your reflection and pictures. You don't see yourself when you laugh. You don't see yourself when you open a gift. You don't see yourself when you pet a dog. We all have things that other people look at and say, "I think that's beautiful", and we might not even acknowledge those qualities about ourselves.

My other best friend is one of my soccer buddies. We've played together for years, but there's always been something I envy about her: that girl can run, and I mean run fast.

We started playing for our school's high school team back in February, but, of course, we had training and practice beforehand.

In the offseason, we did a lot of running. A lot. I was out for six weeks with a knee injury, so obviously I wasn't going to be as fast as her, but I wanted to be. I wanted to be able to sprint up the field as quickly as she could. I craved the praise she would get. It used to tear me apart because I knew I wasn't at the same level she was.

After our season was cut short due to COVID-19, an interview was released where our coach talked about our team.

When he got around to us, I was waiting anxiously to hear what he had to say about my friend. He said something that made me almost angry. I knew he wouldn't say the same about me, but what he did said about me, really opened my eyes. He said I was what he would consider a "utility player", meaning that he could put me on offense or defense and still trust me to be an asset to the victory we were trying to achieve. I was so worried about the great qualities that my friend has, instead of focusing on what makes me a great player. That's when I realized that my friend is really fast and super talented, but that doesn't mean I'm not talented. It's not like there's only a certain amount to go around. We all have our own amount, and we all apply it in different ways. I got caught up in the whole, "I wish I could be like her" factor that I couldn't even recognize what made me the player that I am.

The "I wish" factor is detrimental to your confidence. If you are constantly looking for everyone else's good qualities that you don't have, you won't be able to recognize the ones you *do.*

I posted an Instagram story and asked girls, if they were comfortable with sharing, to tell me some things that they struggled with. One of them particularly caught my eye, and it said "I wish I had a bigger butt." Well, let me tell you, tons of other girls, me included, are right there with you.

I tend to compare myself to people I see on social media. It's like everywhere I click there's a new girl with the "perfect body" that I've been trying to achieve for what feels like forever. Then I have to recognize that those pictures are POSED! I'm not saying posing is a bad thing. Obviously, you're going to pose when someone's taking a picture of you. However, that also means that they don't look like that all the time.

I have a "body positivity" story on my Instagram with all of the girls in my age range. I created it so if they had any current struggles, they wouldn't have to wait for the book to come out. While I was at the beach, I decided to capture what posed vs. unposed looks like: swimsuit style.

In the first picture, I had my bottoms pulled up on my waist, so my waist looked significantly smaller. Then, I sucked in my stomach and flexed my abs, so my abs were visible. Lastly, I turned to the side, so I didn't look as wide. Now, I hardly ever look like that. If I'm at the pool or the beach, and I'm walking around in a bathing suit, I'm not going to do all three of those things. I'm going to look like I usually look. If someone was to take a picture of me, I would probably pull my bottoms up, flex my abs, and turn to the side. Why? So I could pose for the picture; the same picture that might show up on someone's Instagram feed later.

Now, before I get harped on; I understand that some people look like that. However, plenty of people do not without posing.

I used to look at pictures of girls that I saw on Instagram or TikTok, and I would use them as my goal. I was *wishing* to look like them, and I would stop at nothing until I did.

I know girls that edit or facetune their pictures, which makes their pictures even more posed. I just have to remind myself that no one looks like their picture 24/7. I took a picture at the lake in a bathing suit where my stomach was stretched out and I looked totally different. Then I took another sitting down and I was like, "Ah, there she is. There's the stomach I know." So the pictures you're seeing and comparing yourself to are likely not what they look like most of the time.

I recently deleted a popular social media app, TikTok, but I had it for over a year. A few weeks before I deleted it, I saw several posts with girls in swimsuits. I would go through a read the comment section, and I was shocked by what some of the girls had to say. I saw a flood of comments, and most of them were other girls pining after their body. There were even comments that would make the girl feel *guilty* for looking the way she did.

Comparing yourself will break you. Period. If you're constantly looking for things that other people have that you want, it's going to tear you apart inside and blind you from the great things that you have.

Genesis 1 talks about the creation of the world. In the end, God looks at creation and says that it is "Good". In case you weren't already aware, you are a part of God's creation, and God's creation is good, just the way he made it.

I was on the lake the other night just as the sun was setting. It was one of the most gorgeous sunsets I've ever seen. The sky was draped in purples and oranges and I thought to myself, "God painted a pretty sky tonight". Guess what else God painted? You, me, and everything in between. If all of God's creation is beautiful or "good", like the sunsets he paints, how can we turn around and call another part of his creation ugly? That doesn't make sense.

My little sister, who's twelve, was having a rough night with comparing herself to others, and a thought popped into my head. I said:

> "You know how when your teacher gives you a big assignment or project, they also give you a long time to work on it? You know, so your finished piece can look and be perfect?"

She nodded her head and I continued with this:

> "Well, that's kind of how you need to think about yourself. The due date of a project is usually a few weeks after it's presented or announced. God made your due date nine months after you were "presented" because he wanted to use a lot of time to make you perfect. He had this image in his head when he was making you, and now, that's what you are. He doesn't make mistakes. He doesn't have those "oopsie"

or "I didn't mean to do that" moments. Because he *did* mean to do that. Everything about you, God *wanted* to be there. Same thing with your friends. He spent nine months forming them, and, just because you look different, doesn't mean he made a mistake on either one of you."

I saw a quote (I couldn't figure out who wrote it), but it said something similar to: "We can't appreciate beauty if we all looked the same", and that's 100% true. Beauty couldn't exist if everyone and everything looked the same. Beauty is appealing to the eyes, so how could something appeal to our eyes if we saw it everywhere?

Think about it this way; flowers are beautiful. The colors and the way they bloom is breathtaking. Oceans are beautiful too: the water, the creatures that live within, the sound of a wave crashing into the sand; all of it is beautiful. Think about how different flowers and oceans are. They are two totally different things. Are sunsets less beautiful because the ocean has beauty too? Or is an ocean less beautiful because sunsets have beauty too? The answer to both of those is no.

It's not a competition. There's not a certain amount of beauty to go around. It's not the butter you pass around the dinner table, so you don't have to worry about getting a piece. It won't run out before it gets to you. Beauty is distributed evenly. There isn't a scale or system, so why fight for a top spot that doesn't really exist?

chapter 2

"You should look like this."

Society has presented an "ideal body type" for a long time. It changes over time, but we're talking about its current status. If you're comfortable in your body, society is quick to tell you why you shouldn't be. They're saying, "If your body doesn't look like this, it should", and I don't know about you, but I'm about tired of it.

Like I mentioned before, I recently deleted TikTok to detox and, honestly, to help with my comparison issues. I always look at the comments on videos, because some of them, when they aren't derogatory to the creator or anything else, are pretty funny. However, I would come across videos that had comments that were not so funny. Particularly, they were videos of girls who didn't fit the "ideal body type".

Now, this body type is usually called an 'hourglass' body. This means that you have a small waist with curves coming out from that. They also want you to have big breasts and small thighs, but those are just add ons. It's like people are trying to sculpt us and we're pieces of junk if they don't like what they see. So all of these women out there are seeing this and hearing that they *should* look like that or that they *need* to look like that to get the approval of other people.

Now, everyone wants approval. Feeling appreciated or accepted is a natural human desire, but this is over the top. This is telling women that they *won't* be accepted because they don't look a certain way, and that breaks my heart.

Don't get me wrong, there is absolutely nothing wrong with wanting to look like an hourglass. The issues come with the motive.

Do you want an hourglass because that's how *you* want to look? Or do you want an hourglass because someone is telling you that's how you *should* look? Or maybe you do want to look like an hourglass, but is it because you think that's the only way to be accepted? That's inaccurate. Society has enforced certain "rules" onto us. It's like a "this is how to be accepted" class, and I'm dropping out.

I can bet a few people will make comments about how it might be easy to write this book because I am naturally a thin girl. I have a high metabolism, I play sports, and I'm a competitive hula hooper (it's a thing). All of those things, along with my genes, feed into how my body is shaped, so people probably think it's easy for me to talk about confidence and being comfortable with your body. However, I don't fit the " ideal body type" either. Sure, I'm thin, but I don't have a lot of the "requirements". I'm pretty flat-chested. I don't have the round, perky butt that is "needed". I have hip dips, which means that my hips have an indention instead of curving out.

I don't have slim legs. I've played soccer for several years, so my legs are muscular. You see, I don't meet society's standards, but guess what? I'm still valuable. I'm still loved. I'm still worthy. I'm still beautiful.

Now let's talk about working out. Being an athlete, I used to work out every day for about an hour or more. I was really busy with practice and school, so I didn't have a lot of time to look in the mirror. After quarantine started, my routine shifted. I didn't do the normal exercise that I used to, I was stuck at home, and I didn't have to spend as much time on school work. It started messing with my head. I started to get really insecure about my stomach. I hated it. I thought it was too wide and it wasn't flat enough. I started to do four, five, or maybe even six workouts every day, trying to slim down my stomach. I was counting calories, skipping meals, anything to reduce the "fat" on my stomach.

Along with wanting a specific body type, there is also nothing wrong with working out until you look at your motive. Are you working out because you hate your body? Or are you working out because you love your body? I was working out because I hated my body. I wanted to change all of it, and I was determined to do so. Now, I workout because I love my body. I want to make myself stronger so I can improve my athletic ability. I don't just want to look good, I want to *feel* good as well. I want to feel more energized and have more stamina. Now, I am not at all saying that if you don't work out, then you're unhealthy. I just *personally* feel better and healthier when I work out. I used to work out every day, and sometimes even several times a day. Now, I work out every few days. I give myself time to recover.

I'm still not the "ideal body type" that I'm told to be, but I don't want it anymore. I like my body type, and I recognize that it's a normal body type. This made me realize that we need to normalize *every* body type. Skinny is not the "normal". Slim is not the "normal". Short is not the "normal". Tall is not the "normal". Plus-sized is not the "normal". White skin is not the "normal". Dark skin is not the "normal". Every body is a normal body. No health I've ever taken has said that I have to look a certain way to be healthy, because you don't. Society has adapted to the idea that skinny = healthy and plus size = unhealthy. There is not a body type that makes or breaks your value. Every body is a beautiful body, and, I know that can be hard to grasp if you don't have the "ideal body", but it's something we need to recognize.

Society doesn't make the rules. They don't get to determine what is right and wrong when it comes to who we are and what we look like. I'm a girl who doesn't fit hardly any of the requirements to be accepted, but I'm still accepted by everyone around me. So, to me, it sounds like their logic doesn't make a lot of sense. Every body is a normal body, whether society likes it or not.

chapter 3

"You're too..."

Body shaming: probably my least favorite topic. I'm generally a non-confrontational person. I try my best to avoid conflict, and I don't like to shout my opinion at other people, but nothing, and I mean nothing, gets me more fired up than body shaming.

I feel like a lot of people think body-shaming is just "you're too fat", but that's not even close. That doesn't even scratch the surface. "You're too skinny" is just as shameful as "you're too fat." I've had many girls tell me they feel like they are too skinny. It's hard for them to gain weight and they want to. It sounds crazy, but it's actually a very real thing. They want to gain a few pounds so that they have meat on their bones, but, for some girls, it's just difficult.

A lot of people think that "You're too skinny" or even "You're so skinny" is a compliment, but, to some people, it's not. It's like a constant reminder of something you're insecure about and the person bringing it up may have no idea. There are also very many words that you could use in place of "skinny". When people call me "too skinny", I imagine myself as a tree branch or stick, and the sharp edges are my bones sticking out everywhere. However, when people say that I am "slim" or "thin", I don't experience those thoughts. There are just some words that can trigger body hatred. For me, "skinny" is one of them. I also know plenty of girls that think they are too fat. It works both ways, but it's not just that. Body shaming can also be "Your legs are too big", or "Your butt is so flat", or "Your breasts are too big", or "Ew, you have stretch marks?". All of these things are body shaming.

When I was in the 7th grade, I developed a fear of eating in front of other people. I know a lot of girls that are scared to eat in front of boys, but I didn't want to eat in front of anyone, not even my closest friends. I always felt like I ate too much or I ate weird, and I was afraid of being judged. This fear led to a lot of rumors and a lot of jokes made. Even up to this day (I just finished my freshman year of high school), I'm called names like an anorexic, stick, and other derogatory things directed towards my slim appearance. My fear of eating in front of people fizzled out, but I felt like I had to live up to the "anorexic girl" reputation. So when I would eat, it would be in very small amounts. I would lie about what I ate that day. I would tell people I skipped meals when I actually didn't, or I would tell them I ate less than what I really did. I would drop a few pounds when people would ask me how much I weighed, and the list goes on. This all started two years ago, so people don't know how long body shaming can affect someone.

It's also hard to be either/or when it comes to "skinny" vs. "fat". It comes back to the ideal body type. You have to be the perfect amount of everything or you're too much of something else. It's ridiculous. It's like we can never win and it should be considered disgraceful to consider our bodies normal. If you're fat then: "You need to drop a few. No one likes a girl with too much fat on their bodies". However, if you're skinny, then: "Gosh, eat a burger. No one likes skin and bones". Notice how the comments incorporated the phrase "no one likes"? It's all to please other people, but you don't have to win the approval of other people. You are beautiful just the way you are. So you see, body shaming can really go either way. Fat shaming is just what most people think of when they think of body shaming. In reality, body-shaming is any comment diminishing someone's appearance.

When I was in 7th grade, I had someone comment about my acne. A few boys were arguing about where most people get their acne (ex: cheeks, chin, forehead), so they asked me where I got mine. Before I got a chance to answer, one of the boys said, "Reese's is on her chest." The boys erupted with laughter. I was wearing a v-neck shirt, so you could see the red bumps scattered across my skin. I haven't worn that shirt since.

When I was in 8th grade, I had someone tell me I was too flat. They said things like, "Yeah, Reese is cute, but she's flat." After I was body shamed, I would defend myself and tell them that I wasn't flat and I was beautiful just the way I was. They then proceeded to ask me for pictures to "prove" that I wasn't flat. I was hurt. I felt worthless. I felt like an object. After I said no, they photoshopped me onto seductive pictures and sent them around. Again, I was hurt. I felt worthless. I felt like an object, and all of this started with a simple comment about my body.

People really have no idea how long a derogatory comment, joking or not, can stick with someone.

Body shaming can also have a major, but common consequence: an eating disorder. More common in females, eating disorders are destroying and taking the lives of people all across the world. It can have permanent damage, and it can all be started by body shaming.

This is what I'm here to tell you: nobody else's opinion matters. You should be confident in your body because it's *your* body! It's not someone else's body, so other people don't get to make comments or decisions *about* your body. What other people think doesn't determine your value and it shouldn't determine how you view yourself.

Every shameful comment about someone's body is a personal opinion. A lot of people think you are "too" something, and a lot of people feel the need to express that opinion. At the end of the day, their opinion is unimportant. As long as you are in good health, other people's opinions about YOUR body are irrelevant.

A lot of body-shaming comments are based on the idea that your body should look a certain way. People may say that someone is "too fat" because their waist size is thirty inches around instead of twenty-six inches around. People say that someone is "too flat" because they're an A cup instead of a DD. Who determines if someone is "too" something? Is there a rule book that says if you aren't x, y, and z, then you simply have "too much" or "too little" of something? Last time I checked, there wasn't. That being said, when people make comments like that, it's because you don't fit their idea of what you should look like. But, honestly, who cares?

They don't get to have standards about what your body should look like. It's YOUR body! So own it, sister. Your body rocks.

chapter 4

"I'm so ugly."

If you don't know me personally, which I'm assuming most of you don't, I'm not the type to take pictures of myself. I'm not a selfie person unless I'm snapchatting someone, but it only goes to one person. I hardly ever post pictures of myself, simply because I don't take them. And, if I do post pictures of myself, it's because my mom said something like, "Oh my gosh, let me take your picture!". Don't get me wrong, there is absolutely nothing wrong with posting pictures of yourself. I don't *not* do it because I think there's any type of issue with it; I just can never seem to find the right angles or lighting, if I'm being honest. I even hype girls up when they post a selfie.

On Easter of 2020, I decided to post something I never even dreamed of posting. I took three pictures: one for each of my biggest insecurity.

The first picture was a picture of my face. I've been on Accutane for several months now, but, at the time, I had only been on it for about a month or so. My acne and acne scars were still very visible. That was my first insecurity. This was the caption:

> "Acne is a very normal thing, especially for teenagers, but this is one of my top insecurities. Ever since I was in the 6th grade, I've had people tell me how bad my acne is, as if I wasn't already aware. Come around to my freshman year, and I stress out when I leave the house without makeup to cover it up."

My acne is a lot better now, but it's still something I struggle with. It's something that everyone struggles with. I get really bad hormonal acne around my jawline, so right before I menstruate it's like a whole load of breakouts makes their way into town, and it sucks. In the picture, I was turned slightly to the side so I could show everyone where my worst acne patches were, and that was hard. It was hard knowing that all of my friends and followers could see the thing I try so hard to hide.

The next thing I pictured was my stomach.

"Also a very common insecurity, especially for girls. All my life I've been told how thin I am, but I've never been able to let myself believe it. I've done workout after workout, trying to make my stomach completely perfect. I've been called anorexic by my peers because of how obsessed I am with my weight and size."

This also relates to the "ideal body type" subject. Many girls are insecure about their stomachs because they're being told that they should look a certain way, and, the reality is, a lot of us just don't. And guess what? That's okay. We aren't designed to look the same. We're all made differently.

Everything that God says is right and perfect, and he didn't say that every girl should look the same, weigh the same, or wear the same size. Why? Because it's not right and it's not perfect. Again, how can we appreciate and admire beauty if we see the same thing everywhere we go?

The last thing I talked about was my side profile.

"My side profile takes a top insecurity spot because of another insecurity hidden in there: my nose. I've always felt like it's too big and not flattering with my face. I think my glasses make it look even bigger. I also get most of my acne on my cheeks, so this is visible when I am viewed from the side."

There's not much to say about this one. Some people love their side profiles, and some people do not. I do not.

I finished the post with this:

"Psalms 139: 13-14

13 'For you formed my inward parts; you knitted me together in my mother's womb.'

14 'I praise you, for I am fearfully and wonderfully made. Wonderful are your works: my soul knows it very well.' "

While the voice in my head tells me that I'm ugly, God tells me that I am fearfully and wonderfully made. The same God that created the beautiful sunsets and mountains also created me and you. So who am I to say that his creation is ugly? All of his creation is beautiful, including me and you."

When I started struggling with confidence, my parents told me to memorize that verse and meditate on it every time I felt insecure. Let me tell you, it works. Compliments and positive affirmations from people always make me feel good, but true words from the person who created me make me feel even better. I find it easy to doubt the words from my earthly friends and family, but how can I doubt the words from someone who speaks nothing but the truth? So the next time you start to feel ugly, think about what God says vs. what you or even the people around you say. Spoiler alert: God's words always win.

The post is still up on my Instagram if you'd like to see the pictures: (@reesemcca)

c h a p t e r 5

"You're so full of yourself."

Confidence is a very confusing topic, but it doesn't have to be. I've always been told that confidence is attractive, but I've found that confident girls get a lot of hate. Society is telling girls to be confident, but calling them self-absorbed when they are.

Like I said in the previous chapter, I don't tend to post pictures of myself. However, a few weekends ago, I decided to. My family and I were at the lake, and I decided to take a picture with my sister, and she took one of me. Then, I posted both of those to my Instagram. I got the usual girl comments like "You're so pretty!", which, of course, made me feel good. I responded to all of them with some sort of "Thank you" and then proceeded on with my day. I was then scrolling through and saw another "You're so pretty!" comment on one of my friend's posts, but this girl responded with, "No, that's you". That's when I realized something.

I responded "Thank you" to my comments because I agreed with them. I *did* think I looked pretty in the pictures; that's why I posted them. I then found myself feeling a little guilty for agreeing with them, but that's so wrong.

I feel like in today's society, girls aren't allowed to feel confident *or* insecure. If you're confident, then you're "full of yourself" or "self-absorbed". On the other hand, if you're insecure you're "fishing for compliments." So, what can we be? We can't win either way. However, neither of those things are true. We are confident and should be confident because we have a reason to be. We were formed by God, the ultimate king of kings; the one who makes no mistakes. That alone is enough of a reason for us to love ourselves. We should start normalizing women to be confident in themselves.

Also, it's normal to be insecure. I'm insecure. Everyone is insecure about something. I think my nose is too big. I think my stomach is too wide. I think my lips are too small. But notice how all of those started with "I think"? That's because they're personal opinions that I have formed of myself. They aren't actual, true statements. They're just how I view myself.

Like I said earlier, The LORD says I am wonderfully made. Myself, the media, society, and the devil are telling me that I'm not. Who should I believe? Everyone on the outside that's spewing lies? Or the almighty king who knitted and formed together all of my parts and never says anything false? If you didn't notice, that's a rhetorical question. We should believe what the LORD says about us because everything he says is true! Trust me, I know it's difficult, but once you start embracing what the one who created you says, it's a lot easier to ignore the people who didn't.

Think about this. My name is Reese. That's a fact. That is a true statement. My birth certificate says that my name is

Reese Olivia McCallum. Imagine that someone comes up to me and calls me another name like "Ava" or "Maddie", and, when I correct them, they tell me I'm wrong. They tell me that *they* know my name and that *they* are correct. I wouldn't believe them. Why? Because my parents named me Reese. That is legally my name. So why would I let someone who didn't name me influence what I believe? Why would someone who had no creative control in naming me get to decide what my name is? It's the same thing here. Why would I let someone who didn't form my inward parts and knit me together tell me what I should think of myself? That doesn't make much sense.

Being confident is difficult, but we have reasons to be. I'm confident because the LORD made me who I am, but I'm also confident because I love my eyes. I'm confident because I have silky, gorgeous hair. I'm confident because I have pretty teeth that, in turn, give me a pretty smile. So BE

CONFIDENT! Because, let me tell you, *that* looks fabulous

on you.

chapter 6

"That's way too high."

We've all done it. We've all stepped on the scale and hoped for a specific number. We've also all been disappointed when it didn't appear. This is what we've got to understand about weight. All of our weights are made up of different things.

A few months ago, I asked my best friend a simple question: "How much do you weigh?" She's my best friend, like I said, so she didn't have any issue with telling me. I was six pounds heavier than her, and my other best friend weighed less than that, so I saw it as me being the "biggest" of the trio. I was crushed. I didn't want to weigh the same as them; I wanted to weigh less. I wanted to step on the scale and see a number that was lower than theirs, even if it was just by a few decimal points. I skipped meals. I worked out all the time. I drank lemon water to speed up my metabolism. I did everything to drop the weight, and, in the end, I did. I dropped around seven pounds in two weeks. Seven. That's a ridiculous amount of weight loss for someone like me, considering I was almost underweight to begin with (according to my BMI). At the end of the two weeks, it seems like I'd made progress, but I hadn't. I still hated my body. I was still restricting food. I was still working out all the time. `

I was talking to a girl and she asked me who I compared myself to the most. As you might've guessed, I told her my best friends. She then asked me a few questions that I thought were irrelevant to the first question. At the end of the discussion, we'd figured out a few things:

1. My chest is larger

2. My butt is larger

3. I'm taller

4. I'm more hydrated

5. I have more muscle in my legs

Again, I thought all of those facts were irrelevant, until she told me these:

1. Breasts are balls of fat

2. Butt is a lot of muscle

3. The taller I am, the more that steps on the scale

4. Water weight is a thing

5. Muscle weighs more than fat

All of this started to piece itself together in my head. I realized that there's a lot more that goes into the number on the scale. Just because my number is a little higher than somebody else's, doesn't mean it's all fat. I've wanted bigger breasts for a while, and that might be the difference between my weight and my friend's weight. The difference might be a positive thing. I have bigger breasts, so I have added fat, but it's fat that I actually like. I have bigger butt muscles, so there's more of me stepping on the scale, and the same result comes from being tall. My hair is more hydrated, so I might retain more water than her, which in turn adds more weight. I have more muscle in my legs, so I'm adding extra weight there. The difference in our weights could be things that I'm okay with having. It wasn't all fat like I thought it was.

Another "that's way too high" thing I've struggled with is calories. I wasn't taking in a lot of calories, so my soccer coach encouraged me to download a calorie tracker. I could set a goal and track my daily food intake. After several weeks of tracking, I noticed I only took in an average of 800-900 calories every day.

Now, that's a really big number, but when you take it into the right perspective, it really isn't. Healthychildren.org states that female athletes need a minimum of 2,000-2,400 calories a day. I wasn't even taking in *half* what is a healthy *minimum.* I also play soccer: a huge field, no time-outs (except for halftime), and lots of running. Runnersworld.com states that soccer players can run up to seven miles every game. Dr. Daniel V. Vigil says that it is a general rule of thumb that you burn approximately 100 calories for every mile you run. Let's do some math. I was taking in 900 and burning off around 700, and that leaves me with 200. That isn't enough for me to last during the day. Runnersworld.com also states that midfielders can run up to nine and a half miles every game. Guess what? I'm a midfielder. That means I could be burning off more calories than I'm even taking in. Of course,

I'm a youngster on my high school team. I don't play the whole game, but I get plenty of minutes for my age. Either way, I still hadn't set a good intake and burn off ratio when it came to calories, and that had some consequences. I was tired all of the time. I could barely make it through practices. I felt sick all the time, so I didn't want to eat when I got home. This means I would burn off all of these calories and not gain any when I got home. I thought I was being smart, but I was just living an unhealthy lifestyle.

There's also a lot more than calories when it comes to food. A think the "all calories are bad calories" is a misconception that everyone is trying to adapt to. I'm not saying you should get all 2,000+ calories in cookies, but having a cookie isn't the worst thing you can eat. Having a cookie shouldn't result in saying you ate bad that day.

To close, the number doesn't determine anything. So your weight is higher than your friends? As long as you're healthy, it doesn't matter. So the calories in your snack are a little high? Consider the nutrients before you put it back.

Maybe it has added calories because it's high in protein, which

is good for you. Not all calories are "bad calories". Not all

weight is "bad weight".

chapter 7

"Will you be my girlfriend?"

Boys. Like I mentioned before, I asked a lot of my girl-friends to share their biggest insecurities and struggles with me, and, not surprisingly, a lot of them said boys. Now, I'm 15. My friends and I are at the age where we start dating, but it's not always a "slow dance in a parking lot" type of thing. There are hardships. There are ups and downs. There are breakups. There are difficulties that come with boys and choosing to be in a relationship with one.

I'm not saying that every boy is terrible. I'm not sexist. I know us girls can give guys their fair share of issues.

Another thing about boys: finding your value in being with one. When I was younger, I was very, very insecure with how I looked. I had a pretty large friend group of the most gorgeous girls. They had beautiful, long hair and flawless skin. My hair was short and I had acne everywhere. Comparing myself to them came as easy as breathing. It was just something I did naturally. Every boy in school liked them, and I was, well, I was just me.

One day, a boy confessed he had feelings for me. This was not just any boy, though. This was one of the "popular boys". You know, basketball player, cute, friends with all kids in school. I thought he was cute, but I wasn't interested in him in a romantic way. However, I acted like I did. Why? Because I found my value in that. I thought my value was greater because one of *the* boys liked me. Soon, I was referred to as "_____'s girlfriend", instead of "Reese", and that made me proud. I was proud that people associated me with him. Like all young relationships, we broke up, but I went back to thinking that my value wasn't as high as it used to be.

Then something crazy happened. I started to find my value in what the LORD says. I have infinite value because the

LORD says I do, and nothing anyone says or does can change that. No relationship can make or break my value.

Let's find my birth certificate again. My middle name is Olivia. It says it on there. Say someone says my name is "Reese Anne" instead. They try to change a little part of it. That's still not right. They don't get to determine any part of it, whether they agree with some of it or not. Maybe they treat me with little value, but they think it's okay because they agree I have *some* value. My parents named me Reese Olivia, and nothing is going to change that. The LORD says I have infinite value, and nothing is going to change that.

Finding your value in what the LORD says is really helpful.

Finding your value in a boy isn't the only hard habit to fall into; pleasing them is one, as well.

I made a promise to myself when I was younger that I would save myself for marriage. But, to me, that's not just sex.

I'm saving me. I'm saving my body for marriage, not just intercourse. It's my body. No one gets to see it but me. Just because you are a boyfriend, absolutely does not mean you get the *right* to see it. Because that's what it is. It's a privilege. A privilege reserved for my future husband and no one else.

A lot of boys, not all, are looking for a physical relationship instead of an emotional one, and they'll tell you anything you want to hear to get it from you. That's why boundaries are so important.

It's a hard and awkward conversation, but it's one you need to have. Boundaries aren't just about a boy respecting you, it's also about you respecting yourself. That's why there's just certain things I don't do. I don't snapchat people in the shower. I don't wear revealing clothing. I don't send seductive or inappropriate pictures of myself. It's because I respect myself. I know that my body isn't for everyone. It's for me until I get to share it with my husband. I realize that my body is precious, and it's not meant to be just thrown around.

There's also temptations, and not just for guys. It's crazy how one thing can lead to another, and it might all start with a touch. This book is mainly about loving your body, but respecting it is just as important. It's not the bread basket at the dinner table; not everyone gets a piece. It is not an object to be tampered with.

I've been objectified. I know girls who've been objectified. It's awful, but it's common. This is what I had to tell myself. I am not an object. I am a human being. I am a woman. I am beautiful. I am more than my body. Read that out loud to yourself, because all of it is true.

Here's the deal: boys have hormones. Girls do too, but guys' minds tend to wander when it comes to the physical stuff. Like I said, a lot of boys, but not every one, are on the lookout for one thing. I don't think I need any further explanation. Here's what you need to understand: you are more than what you have been treated as. Remember that, then no guy can turn you into an object because you've already established and made clear that you're not.

Proverbs 3:15

"She is more precious than rubies; nothing you desire can compare with her."

If you had a precious ruby or gem, would you let just anyone hold it? Would you leave it out for everyone to mess with? Or would you keep it safe? Protected? Guarded?

I don't know about you, but I would keep my gem safe, clean, guarded, and protected. Something so beautiful and precious deserves to be treated as such.

Now think about this: the LORD says we are even *more* precious than that. Think of how much you'd take care of something like that.

You are valuable, whether a guy says you are or not. You are more than your body. You are all of these amazing things, but one thing you aren't is an object. Do not let a guy treat

you like one.

chapter 8

"New diet starts today."

When I was little, I had a plan for what I wanted to do when I grew up. I wanted to go to Harvard, be a neurosurgeon, play professional soccer, and be a published author. It took me a while to realize that those goals were simply unrealistic.

So let's talk about goals, and why some of them just don't make sense.. A lot of goals are influenced by social media and other people. They've established some sort of checklist, and if you don't check all of the boxes, then you're not good enough.

Society wants you to have big breasts, a big butt, a flat stomach, small legs, clear skin, and a small number when you step on the scale. Some of those things can't work hand in hand.

Your butt is made up of a bunch of muscles, and, to grow a bigger or rounder butt, you have to work and strengthen those muscles. If you don't know already, muscle weighs more than fat. Say you step on the scale on July 1st and weigh 124.7 pounds. Then, on July 15th, you step on the scale and weigh a little bit more. That doesn't mean it's fat. That shouldn't be what you automatically assume. Maybe your butt got bigger. All of this to say, if you have a larger butt, your number will increase. There's more of you stepping on the scale.

I've always been very flat-chested, and many comments have been made about that. So, I guess you could say, I don't fit society's standards. I don't fill bathing suits or some tank tops, and *I'm* okay with that, but society isn't. My mom has always told me that if I gain weight, it would start to be evident in my chest. But remember what society says? You can't weigh a lot. It *has* to be a small number. But you also must have big breasts. Guess what breasts are? Balls of fat. I said earlier than muscle weighs more than fat, but, obviously, fat still adds some.

I have a question, society. How are we supposed to have balls of fat on our chest and big, strong muscles in our butt, but *still* manage to keep a lower number? While you come up with an answer, I'm going to finish talking.

Another thing about goals is the time it takes to achieve them. A lot of workout videos say that you can get _____ in _____ amount of time. Then the picture or thumbnail they show is an image of whatever you're trying to achieve by doing the workout, (ex. abs, legs, arms, etc.). But, when you do them for whatever time it says, you don't see results. Then what?

You have to think about the starting point because everyone's starting point is different. Let's say I'm looking at doing an abs program. I have some love handles and a little bit of stomach fat. Let's say another girl wants to do the same one. She has a flat stomach, but she just wants her abs to show a little more. We do the same workout for the same amount of time. Who is going to look more like the thumbnail? Probably the other girl. Why? Because her starting point was a lot different than mine. If I still get results, that's all that matters. You can't always expect to look like the picture. It's unrealistic. Your starting point is going to be different. Our bodies are like snowflakes: we might look similar, but no two bodies are the same. Some people just need a little more time to get the results that are advertised, and that's totally okay. If someone gets results faster, that doesn't mean there is anything wrong with you.

You should set your own goals. When I was working out because I hated my body, my goal was to be "slim thick" because that's what I saw everywhere. I wasn't doing it for me; I was doing it for everyone else. Now that I workout because I love my body, my personal goal is to get stronger so that I can be a better soccer player. I used to work out every day, pushing myself to do things that I just couldn't do. I'd workout several times a day, even if I was exhausted. Now, I don't work out every day. Sometimes I skip a day. Sometimes I skip two. If I'm in the middle of a workout and I just can't do it, I'll stop. I'm a lot happier now. Setting your own goals will relieve so much stress. Trying to achieve society's goals feels like reaching for something that you just aren't tall enough to grab. It's exhausting and unrealistic.

chapter 9

"I'm not hungry."

I've said this phrase many times. A while ago, one of my "hidden talents" was ignoring my hunger pains. After a while, I had trained my body not to recognize them. I couldn't figure out when I was hungry.

Guess what I just did? I stopped writing because I was hungry. I had some chicken and apples. Guess what else? I'm still hungry, so maybe I'll make something else. Guess what else? (the finale). All of that is okay.

So here I am, eating a bowl of soup, telling you that it is okay. Eating a snack after a meal because your body is still hungry is okay. Eating something your craving is okay. Eating a whole pint of ice cream on your period is okay. All of that is okay.

You need to listen to your body because she knows what she's talking about. She knows if she's hungry and needs food. Of course, you have to be smart with what you're eating, but listening to your body is a good thing. It's a *smart* thing. It's a *healthy* thing.

It's also okay to be bloated. One of my favorite fitness trainers, Chloe Ting, posted a picture of her stomach the other day. A lot of the pictures on her feed are pictures of her *very visible* abs, but this picture was different. She was bloated, and she's a fitness trainer. I'm not saying that it's unheard of or unusual for a fitness trainer to be bloated; it's actually very normal. What I am saying is that you shouldn't tear yourself up when you're bloated. Everyone gets bloated. People who work out and eat healthy get bloated. I get bloated right before and during my period. I get bloated after I drink a certain coffee. I get bloated whenever I'm under a lot of stress. I even get bloated after eating certain food. See, a lot of people think that I am always slim and tiny, but, in reality, my stomach likes to pop out to say hello from time to time.

I used to look at myself in the mirror when I was bloated and I would criticize myself.

"You shouldn't look like that."

"You need to skip dinner."

"You're supposed to be skinny."

"You're so fat."

"_____ doesn't look like that."

"You need to go workout again."

None of those things are true or accurate. NONE But, I convinced myself they were because I said them over and over again.

I used to get mad at myself when I ate a snack. I thought it was too much, when, in reality, my stomach needed it. But you know what I did after? I'd go burn it all off. Again, I thought it was a smart lifestyle. If I burned off the same amount of calories I took in, I wouldn't gain any weight, right? Wrong. That is so unhealthy. I had no energy. I was dizzy. I would lay in bed all the time. I felt sick. I had trouble sleeping. It was the most exhausting thing I've ever endured, but I thought I was helping myself.

So listen to your body. She may be a little sassy because she knows what she wants and when she wants it, but, unlike little girls, it's a *good* idea to give her what she's asking for. Think of her as a puppy. If she's hungry, feed her, and don't take her on a walk right after to burn off the calories.

chapter 10

"You look pretty today."

I've always been told I'm awful at accepting compliments. No matter what, I'll always have some sort of rebuttal to tell you while you're wrong. It used to blow my mind that people thought I was pretty because I didn't at all.

A few months ago, I decided to track how many times I looked in the mirror. I used my notes app and added a point every time I lifted my shirt to see my stomach. 30-40 times. I usually spend around 5-10 seconds. That means I could be spending up to 6+ minutes just staring at myself. It doesn't seem like a lot of time, considering there are 24 hours in a day, but the fact that I'm spending six whole minutes staring at myself and criticizing what I see, is alarming. I would do it every morning, excited to see my "morning skinny" and a small waist. Then I would do it every time I passed my mirror.

Picture this: I roll out of bed, probably around 11:00 because I'm a late sleeper, and I go straight to the mirror, I lift up my shirt and twist and turn. I turn towards the natural light and squeeze my abs, trying to make my stomach as flat as possible. I see my "morning skinny" and I'm happy. This is what sets the tone for the morning. I am happy because I look thin, instead of being happy for better reasons.

A lot has changed since then. Now, when I lift my shirt, I'm okay with how I look. I don't twist and turn to change how I look. I look at myself straight on; no sucking in, no turning to the side, no flexing. Not much has changed on the outside. It's the inside that's experienced a difference. If and when I saw myself, I would speak only *positive* things. And, let me tell you, that has made a world of a difference.

Compliments aren't just about complimenting other people. It's okay to compliment yourself. Like I said earlier, society finds it odd when girls are confident in themselves, and they consider it "self-absorbed", but it's not. It's actually healthy to look at yourself and say, "You look pretty today."

I tried an exercise for a while, and I definitely recommend trying it if you criticize yourself every time you see your reflection. For every one thing you don't like about yourself, name three things that you do. It's almost forcing you to change perspective and find things that you like. If you can't name things you like, then you can't name things you don't. I wouldn't leave my reflection until I found things that I liked instead, and, by that time, I'd pretty much forgotten what I'd criticized in the first place. It created a newfound love for myself. It's a healthy way to acknowledge insecurities, but realize that there are other things besides them.

Another thing to practice, waking up positive. I used to go to the mirror every single morning, as soon as I woke up, and criticize myself. I'd lift my shirt, see my stomach, and spout out all the things I hated about it. Now, I don't lift my shirt. I look at myself and say, "Reese, you look beautiful today." It's a good way to start your day off. I also have a sticky note above my mirror that reads "See why Jesus died". It's a daily reminder that he died for the girl in the mirror, and I look different every time I look in the mirror. I could be in my pj's, dressed up, dressed down, crying, sick, or a full face of makeup, but Jesus died for me. He died for the girl in the mirror and everyone else that looks in it. So I also encourage you to try that to shift your thinking, because how crazy is it to think that someone thought you were so amazing that they shed their blood for you? Pretty cool, if you ask me.

The first night we were at the beach, we went to dinner near our hotel. I was wearing a super cute black shirt that tied in the side, but you could see my stomach. I got several weird looks, but guess what? I didn't care. I looked in the mirror and thought myself and my outfit looked *beautiful.* So, in the end, it didn't bother me if other people disagreed. That's their problem. I don't care what other people think about me, because they don't get to determine how I see myself. I already know I'm beautiful. Why do I need anyone else's opinion?

I like to try to compliment people everyday, but it's important to extend yourself the same courtesy. Positive thinking creates a mindset shift, which could totally change how you see the girl in the mirror.

chapter 11

"Girl, you're stunning."

One time, I was at Chick-fil-a with my grandma and there was a bumper sticker on a car that said "Babes support babes" in pink lettering. My grandmas asked what "babies support babies" meant, and I had to explain to her that it meant "girls support girls", after laughing at her, of course. Then, I thought about what that means. What does it mean to be a girl that supports girls?

Supporting other girls can be difficult because of the "I wish" factor. Have you ever run for a position at your school? Maybe it's a student council position or a team captain. Have you ever been beat? If you have, then think back to how you felt. If you haven't, try to imagine how you would feel. I have, and it was really hard for me to support the person who beat me because *they* had what *I* wanted.

Supporting girls can be hard when they have what you desire to have. Maybe it's a flat stomach. Maybe it's unbelievably clear skin. Maybe it's freckles. I find it difficult to support girls that have those things. Let's talk about why we should, though.

Society is starting to normalize girl vs. girl. All of these girls compete with each other. We're all fighting for those Instagram comments and it's ridiculous. We need a mindset shift. We need to start acting like a team.

It's insane what we girls can do. In Genesis, we learn that the first woman was created from the rib of another human being. We can form literal humans inside of our bodies. Heck, we can bleed for several days straight and *not* die. How cool is that?

I love Instagram because I can comment on other girls' posts and hype them up. It's one of my favorite things about the app. I love when girls comment on my post, so, in turn, I do it too. You might not realize how much of an impact that can have on someone's day.

We need to start supporting each other. Society has compared girls to other girls for years, so it's natural to do it personally, but that doesn't mean it's right. If we would start being happy for other girls, life could be a whole lot simpler. We also need to support each other because it's a tough world out there. I've heard several stories about how girls get catcalled and another girl comes up to her and acts as if they're friends so the guy will leave her alone. There's a prime example of why us girls have got to stick together. Catcalling, sex trafficking, and tons of negative attention are mainly targeted towards females. We've got to stick together and stick up for each other.

That being said, I get it. It's difficult. I'm not an angry person. I'm usually happy and bubbly; people even tell me that I remind them of the color yellow. However, a while ago, I used to be infuriated when I saw girls with the "ideal body" that I was pining for. Outraged.

"Why don't I look like that?"

"How did she do that?"

"*I wish* I could look like that." (There's that "I wish" factor again)

"How come she looks like that and I don't?"

Constant comparison. It tore me apart. I worked out almost every day and ate relatively healthy (until it came to any sort of cookie), but she still looked better than me. That angered me. That led to working out more, eating less, and a lot of self-hatred. But it wasn't just me that I was criticizing. That also led to some reverse comparison.

"Well, I have less acne."

"At least my thighs aren't that big."

"Her breasts are smaller than mine."

"My hair looks better."

"Her teeth are crooked."

I tore *her* down to make *me* feel better. Reverse comparison is just as unhealthy as a regular comparison. Sure it made me feel better in the moment, like I had won, but in the end, I would just hate myself even more because what I had wasn't *enough.*

Now, supporting girls comes naturally, and it's fun. I've made a lot more friends. I've helped a lot of people and a lot of people have helped me. So you see, supporting girls is hard sometimes, but it's an amazing and beautiful thing when you learn how to. We're a team. We're knocked down by sexism and traditions, so, maybe if we learn to work together, we can show the world just how powerful we are.

chapter 12

"She's cute, but..."

Society Rules: part 12. You cannot be beautiful *because* of your differences. You must be beautiful *in spite* of them.

I feel like this is a very common one and it's a very easy habit to pick up.

"She's cute, but she's fat."

"She's cute, but her breasts are small."

"She's cute, but her butt is flat."

"She's cute, but she has a lot of acne."

The "She's cute, but" issue. This is an issue that results from normalizing one specific body type. It sounds almost painful for people to admit that a girl is pretty despite her "flaws". But this is my question: Who decided that those were flaws? Who decided that those were bad things? Is there a rulebook or a handbook I missed out on. Last time I checked, those are normal things.

I mentioned this earlier, but I'm going to touch on it again. I talked to a guy in 7th grade, and a year later he admitted that his friends would say things like, "Yeah, Reese is cute, but she's flat".

Now, he wasn't wrong in saying that. I've even been called printer paper at times, (but I can sleep on my stomach, so who's the real winner here?), and it's hurtful. It bothered me that my "prettiness" couldn't also include the fact that I am flat. Why is it either? Why can't I just be both?

I feel like a lot of this book sounds like I'm dragging everyone and I'm little Miss Perfect who does nothing wrong, but that is entirely false. I find myself doing this as well.

I saw a swimsuit ad the other day on Instagram, and the first thing I noticed was her body figure: I would consider her plus-sized. Here's where I had to stop myself. It was a video, so when they showed her face, I was genuinely shocked at how gorgeous she was. She had a beautiful smile and long, healthy-looking hair. So what made me surprised that she was pretty? Why was I in shock? The standards. We are told, normalizing, and believing that to be pretty, you must first be skinny. We are told, normalizing, and believing that to be pretty, you must have small thighs. We are told, normalizing, and believing that to be pretty, you must first have a small waist. That's not all, though. You don't want everything to be small. You have to make sure those breasts and butt are nice and perky, but not too big, you don't want to be giving off the wrong idea. Make sure they're a little smaller than that, but not too small, you have to have a little something to show.

I don't know about you, but, to me at least, that's confusing. We're all okay with society's standard list because no one has actually laid it out like that, and that's not even all of it. You need to have clear, smooth skin. Your hair needs to look nice and healthy. No dark circles. You have to be clean and proper. You need perfect makeup, but still natural; no one likes a cakey face.

That's awful. It's confusing. It's hard to keep up with. It's unrealistic. It makes no sense. So why are we enforcing it? Why are we raising girls to believe that they will never be enough unless they check all the boxes? We are teaching them from a young age that they can *only look* a certain way, or they won't be accepted.

I love stores like American Eagle and Aerie because they advertise realistic bodies. There are all shapes, sizes, and skin tones. It's beautiful. It is beautiful to see all of us girls accepted, and especially in bathing suits. They are accepted showing off skin. They are accepted as they are.

Social media and society are setting unrealistic goals that we females will never be able to achieve.

I have a very funny soccer coach. He'll say something like "You have to make it to the end of the field in three seconds". That's impossible. It would be insane if he were to actually hold us accountable for that. Well, society is telling us that we have to make it to the end of the field in three seconds, and they're being serious. We can't leave practice until we reach that goal, but it's impossible. We're wearing ourselves out trying to reach something that's simply unachievable.

These aren't flaws. These are *differences.* These are *unique.* These are the things that make everyone's beauty different. So she is pretty. She's not pretty *despite* what you consider "flaws". She's stunning, and that includes them.

chapter 13

"I think I'm in love."

We've all said this phrase. I think I've even said it more than once. "I think I'm in love."

A while ago, I was struggling with the guy I was "dating" or whatever we did in middle school. I always felt like I got on his nerves. We were really bad at communicating together. And, I would later find out, that we just weren't the right fit. Also around this time, I was really struggling with self-image. I hated the way I looked. I thought I was ugly, and I thought everyone around me was drop-dead gorgeous. "What am I doing wrong?" was a constant thought that circulated throughout my brain, because that's how I felt. I thought I was doing something incorrectly. I thought I had some kind of disadvantage that made my value lesser than the beautiful girls around me. Flash forward almost three years, and I don't feel the way. It's not because I think the other girls aren't as pretty as I thought they were; it's because I realized that I'm pretty too. I realized my value.

I had a friend tell me during this time something very simple, yet very effective.

"You've got to learn to love yourself before you can love someone else."

At first, I thought it was probably just a random quote she saw on VSCO or Instagram, then I started thinking about it.

If you are reading this and don't know my story (or even me personally), then you don't know my past when it comes to guys. I'm not going to use this book to drag boys or publicly shame them, but I have had plenty of road bumps when it comes to guys. I haven't been treated well. I haven't been treated like I should've been treated. I've been lied to, manipulated, body shamed, knocked down, and all sorts of things that honestly shape me into the woman I am today. It caused me to mature a little bit earlier than everyone else around me. It showed me heartbreak at an early age, and not the kind of heartbreak where they break up with me and we part ways. This was the kind of heartbreak that made me question if I was ever going to be worthy enough. This was the kind that made me surprised when people complimented me because I thought I was just *that* ugly. The heartbreak didn't result in me hating them; it resulted in me hating myself.

You may be asking yourself a few questions. I asked myself the same. Why did I stay in a relationship with someone who didn't treat me right? Why did I let that relationship tear me apart? Why, why, why? I didn't know for a while, but I finally figured it out a few months ago. How can I influence how another guy treats me? Let me show you.

Obviously, I didn't have any part in how the guy treated me. I had a part in *why*. Why did he continue to? It's because I never stood up for myself. In my eyes, I had little value, so I thought I deserved to be treated that way. I thought I deserved to be treated as if I had no value, so I let them do it. I let them walk all over me. I let them hurt me time and time again. I let them spit on me. That's what I deserved, right?

Wrong.

Around this time, I was finding my value in what I saw around me. Who was prettier than me? Who had more friends? Who was more popular? Who was better at sports? All of those questions, and more, tallied into what I thought of myself. It was almost like a game with a scoring system, and I couldn't seem to make any shots.

So I was okay with how they treated me. I saw myself as worthless, so when they treated me that way it felt normal. It felt deserved, but, girl, was I wrong.

My point of view totally changed when I found my value in something else. I started finding my value in what the creator says about me, instead of the other 'created'.

Finding your value in what the creator says is the only way to see how much you really have. Otherwise, it's all just a hierarchy system. People are higher than others, and people are lower than others. You get points depending on if you have more or less of something. You compare your everything to somebody else's everything, and the scale goes up or down. We are all numbered, and we are in a line from top to bottom. When you acknowledge that the creator determines your value, you realize that there isn't a hierarchy. We're aren't numbered. We're all in a straight line because we're all equal.

I saw my value at the end of the hierarchy line. I was towards the bottom because I thought of my value as little to none. I thought I was ugly. I thought I was worthless. So, in the end, I let guys treat me that way.

My friend was right. I had to learn to love myself before I tried to love someone else, and before I let someone else love me. They treated me like I was the value I thought I had, not the value I actually am. In turn, I experienced a lot of heartbreak because of it. A lot of people our age are so obsessed with romantic love, that we forget how important self-love is.

I know I'm only 15, but here's my advice: Learn your value before you let someone treat you like it's less than it is.

chapter 14

"You're beautiful."

Surrounding yourself with people who will continually repeat this phrase is important because there's a difference between fishing for compliments and *actually* feeling insecure.

I know girls who love to fish for compliments. They wake up extra early to fix their hair and makeup and still say "Oh my gosh, I look so ugly", just so they can know that someone recognizes that they look good. I do this too. Tons of people do. Everyone wants to hear a compliment, even if you have to pry it out of someone. That's why it's important to surround yourself with people who will build you up, without forcing it out of them or having to ask for it.

I just got back from the beach last night, and the first thing I did was fall back into an old habit: looking at myself in the mirror. Our condo didn't have a full-length mirror, so I didn't get to see myself like I usually do for several days. It was very refreshing. I brought several cropped shirts, so I was worried about other people seeing my biggest insecurity, but I couldn't see it. I didn't worry about it all week. We ate out every night, and I ate all of it most of the time. I was about to start my period, so I had a lot of chocolate. I drank a lot of water, but I had 2 or 3 sweet teas. Needless to say, with all the eating and the bloating, I felt like I looked so much bigger when I got home. I was upset. I was mad at myself.

A few months ago, I realized there's a thing called body dysmorphia. It's where you genuinely can't see yourself the way other people see you. The people around me get so frustrated when I call myself "fat" or "huge" because they see something that I can't.

Last night, my friend could tell I was upset. He asked me what was wrong, and I told him I just felt ugly. Not thirty seconds later, I get a phone call. I answered, and he told me to listen. He talked for at least three minutes straight. He complimented me and listed off things he liked about me, but there was one particular phrase that stood out.

"I know you see _____, but everyone else, including myself, sees _____."

That phrase caught my attention. He told me that what I see is not what everyone else sees and he was right.

You don't have to have body dysmorphia for this to apply to you, too. Sometimes we just get blinded by our insecurities. It's like they're the biggest thing in the mirror, and it's the first thing our eyes dart to. After that, it's the only thing we see. It's important to surround yourself with people who will not only build you up, but also understand that you may not see what they see.

Along with complimenting others, we also have to be careful with how we present them. I had someone bring this to my attention the other day, and it really made me stop and question how I was making other people feel.

Stop calling yourself _____ around people that are _____er than you.

If you're around people that are considered plus-sized and you're not, don't call yourself fat. If you're around someone with noticeably smaller breasts than you, don't say that your breasts are too small. I've done that without even realizing it. A lot of people have.

I've called myself "fat" or "huge" around people who weren't that either, but they were bigger than me. Think about how that makes them feel? If someone smaller than them is "so fat", then what are they? What are *we* calling *them?*

Then we do the thing where we try to reverse it.

"Omg girl, you're so skinny!"

So, if she's bigger than you, but you're "so fat" how can you call her skinny? Or maybe you do believe she's skinny, but you're smaller than her, so how can you be fat? It doesn't add up because it doesn't make sense. Criticizing yourself doesn't only hurt you, it can also hurt the people around you. It has several negative effects and no positive ones.

So how do we compliment others?

A part of my personality is being a people-pleaser. I love giving gifts, seeing people happy, *making* people happy, and doing anything to see their faces light up. That's why compliments, even if I'm terrible at accepting them sometimes, are one of my favorite things. I love giving them out because I've noticed that they can totally shift someone's day around. One of my favorite editing apps, VSCO, is where I love to give compliments. I love it because there are no likes, comments, or follower numbers. You can't see how much of something someone else gets, so there's not a lot of comparison on the app. However, since you can't comment on their pictures, I like to message them privately and tell them that I think they're really pretty. I don't know them and they don't know me, but it takes 5 seconds to make someone's day. Why not compliment someone? It's easy, free, and it takes hardly any time. It also makes me feel better. It makes *me* feel good knowing that I made *someone else* feel good.

Imagine if you gave out just one compliment every day. Imagine how that positivity can spread because when someone compliments me, I feel compelled to compliment someone else because I want them to feel that joy too. Something so simple can make such an impact, so start doing something simple, even if it's just once a day.

Along with giving compliments (in the right way), we should also start learning to accept them when they are given to us. In one of the earlier chapters, I talked about how I felt almost guilty when I responded with a simple "Thank you."

"You're, like, really pretty."

"Thank you."

"So, you agree?"

"What?"

"You think you're really pretty?"

"Oh, I don't know."

Recognize this? If you don't, let me explain. This is a scene from the movie Mean Girls. A girl compliments another girl, and it almost sounds like she's trying to make her feel guilty for agreeing. It's just a scene in a movie, and she's considered the "meanest mean girl", so it's all scripted. However, we need to realize that it's not always scripted. I felt bad saying "thank you" because I felt rude for agreeing with them. The thing is; I did agree with them. I wouldn't have posted the pictures if I didn't think I looked pretty in them. So why did I feel so weird about agreeing with them?

Posting selfies or pictures of yourself doesn't make you self absorbed, and agreeing that you're pretty doesn't either. I'm not saying that a response to a compliment should be "I know", but it's okay to politely agree because it's true. We need to start normalizing accepting compliments because that's what they're intended for. They aren't there to be argued about.

"No, I'm not."

"I'm really not."

"No, that's you."

Accept them. That's what they're meant for. Even if you don't agree, if you accept them, and I mean really accept them, you might start to. Someone wouldn't compliment you if they didn't mean it. That would just be a waste of time, wouldn't it?

Compliments are uncomfortable sometimes. I'm horrible at accepting compliments sometimes, but, the more I accept, the more I start to believe. You shouldn't feel guilty. So the next time someone compliments you, just accept it. In the end, it's easier, and it might help you start to believe them about yourself.

chapter 15

"No junk food."

We've all heard this phrase. Whether it be from a coach or our own brains, we've all had this phrase thrown at us.

Now, I don't know about you, but I've got a major sweet tooth: ice cream, cookies, chocolate, etc. If it has sugar, you can bet I'll have no trouble eating it. That's not all, though. Sweet tea? Love it. Soda? Love it. If you don't get it, I'm basically in love with sweet stuff. The issue? I'm an athlete.

I've mentioned a few times before that I'm a soccer player, but I haven't said much other than that. I used to practice almost every day in the fall for off-season training (except for my break due to an injury), and almost every day in the winter and going into spring. Needless to say, all of that work and energy wasn't fueled off of junk food. I hate to eat high protein meals, drink water, and steer away from foods that would give me a sugar crash. That being said, I did *not* restrict those foods all the time. I'd have an occasional soda or glass of tea. I'm big on baking, so I'd make cookies and cakes and eat those too.

When the season came around, I had to be really intentional about what I ate. I'd have high carb meals like pasta nights before a game. I'd have lots of water throughout the day. I'd have fruit or some kind of healthy snack before the game. Our coaches weren't super strict about eating, as in they didn't monitor, but they did talk to us about smart and intentional eating.

I had one of my good friends message me the other day and tell me that she has personally been struggling with the "no junk food" mindset. She's an athlete, and she says her coaches have also stressed the importance of smart eating choices while training. However, her mindset is that she can't have *any* junk food. Her coaches are saying she has to stay in shape, which is important, but her mind is telling her that she's not allowed to eat anything that could be considered "junk" or even "unhealthy" food.

Let's talk about restrictions. Restricting isn't just limiting your intake of food; it can also be limiting the amount of certain foods.

A while ago, I was struggling with my relationship with food. I didn't eat as much as I needed to. I thought I had to eat super healthy foods all of the time to "stay in shape", and I would feel guilty if I had something high in sugar or fat. I developed an unhealthy relationship with calories.

This is what I'm here to tell you.

"In shape" comes in all shapes.

Business Insider asked Shawn Arent, an exercise scientist at Rutgers University, what "in shape" really meant. His response:

"There is no one definition. It can be everything from having low body fat to having good cardiovascular endurance to having muscular strength — to be pain free, to be stress free, all these things ... and I really think it depends on what the person's goals are.

"It depends on what you're trying to do. If you're trying to run a marathon, your version of in shape might be something very different than someone competing in a body building contest or someone that plays flag football on the weekend.

"Generally the way we define it is that your cardiovascular endurance — your cardiorespiratory endurance — is good enough that you don't easily get winded. So your VO2 max is above average, in terms of oxygen consumption.

"[Being in shape can also mean] having a good level of body fat — I don't want to say low — because obviously you don't want to go too low with body fat (there's other problems there), but a healthy [level of] body fat is probably the best

way to look at it. Where you're considered lean, most people consider that "in shape." So like I said it really depends on what your goals are ...

"... It just depends on what you want your shape to be."

Stamina is a common goal when it comes to staying or being "in shape". But what is stamina?

Stamina is having energy and physical ability to survive prolonged physical activity. Healthline.com lists 5 ways to achieve stamina.

1. **Exercise**

2. **Yoga & Meditation**

3. **Listening to music**

4. **Caffeine**

5. **Ashwagandha (It's a thing I swear. It's an herb)**

Now tell me where it says that you should restrict "junk" foods? I'll wait.

I'm a soccer player, particularly a midfielder, so stamina is an important aspect for me being in shape. I recently had a club tryout, and I did not do as well as I usually do. It was hot, humid, and I couldn't seem to get through drills without being exhausted. A lot of girls made comments on how they were out of shape, and it was for the same reason. It wasn't because we looked a certain way.

We were just tired and couldn't get through the long drills. Our bodies are different, but we were all out of shape from not playing since March.

Healthy and intentional eating ≠ restricting junk food

Slim doesn't not always mean that you are in shape.

chapter 16

"She's so kind"

A lot of this book has focused on outward beauty, but let's talk about inward beauty.

I have always been raised to be kind to everyone, even if I don't want to be. I used to be so worried about my outward appearance, that the way I presented my inward beauty seemed irrelevant to me. As long as I was pretty on the outside, I was fine, right? Wrong.

Think of your favorite dessert. Personally, mine is chocolate cake. Say there's a beautiful chocolate cake sitting in front of me, but it tastes awful? Would I still eat it? No. why? Just because the outside is nice, doesn't mean the inside is, and the inside is what matters, right?

I know girls who are drop-dead gorgeous, but their personality isn't. At the end of the day, it doesn't matter how beautiful your face is; it's the beauty of your heart that's so important. A pretty face will fade, but a pretty heart will always be remembered.

I wrote this book to make you more comfortable with your outward appearance, not to tell you that it's the most important kind of beauty. It's important to acknowledge your outward beauty, but it's crucial to exhibit inward beauty.

I don't know about you, but compliments always feel better when they're directed towards my personality. I'd much rather be called kind than pretty. As a girl, I'm not going to force myself to hang around pretty girls if they're going to be rude to me. I'd much rather hang around girls who don't fit the "beauty standards", but are kind. Inward beauty makes your outward beauty even more evident.

A while ago, I told my mom all the things I wish I had that the people around me did. I wanted a bigger chest. I wanted a rounder, perkier butt. I wanted less acne. I wanted slimmer thighs. She listened and then asked me if I thought anyone said those things about me. Did I think that anyone wanted what I had? I told her that most of my compliments are directed at my kindness. I've been told I'm a good listener. I give great advice. I'm everyone's friend. I'm just naturally a nice person.

She told me that it was those things that mattered the most. She told me that when we get older, we won't remember the pretty girls. We'll remember the girls who welcomed us with kindness. We'll remember the girls who were kind to us. We'll remember the girls who accepted us. We'll remember the girls who were always uplifting.

Think of it like this. There are two kinds of lipstick. There's the lipstick that comes off of my lips as soon as I take a sip of water, and there's the lipstick that literally stays on for days. Outward beauty is the first lipstick. It fades. It doesn't stick with people. It doesn't show for long. Inward beauty is the second. It stays. It's bright and everyone can see it for a long time. People remember what color it was because it didn't fade after a few hours.

Inward beauty is still beauty, whether it's appealing to the eyes, or not.

apter 17

'Just the way you are."

This might be one of the most important topics in the book, so, if you don't read any other chapter, at least read this one.

I've mentioned this quote several times, but I think we need to really unpack it. Again, I am unsure of who wrote it, considering I saw it on VSCO, but, whoever it was really knows what they're talking about.

"We couldn't appreciate beauty if we all looked the same."

Think about that. We think things are beautiful because of the way they look. They look different from other things. Like I said earlier, in my personal opinion, I think flowers and oceans are the most gorgeous aspects of nature, but they're two different things. Oceans are a form of water. The way the waves crash into the sand and the creatures that live beneath the depths are amazing. Flowers are also beautiful. They way they can come from a seed and prosper into beautiful petals. Totally different things. Totally beautiful. Now let's shift perspective. Let's use people as an example. (P.S. this is the ONLY kind of comparison in this book)

There's me.

My name is Reese McCallum. I'm 15. I wear a size medium in shirts. I'm about 5'6". I'm caucasian. I've got glasses, but sometimes I wear contacts. I'm a blonde, but my hair color is currently strawberry blonde from a recent dye. I've got dark blue eyes. I do soccer, FBLA, I'm in student council, and a competitive hula hooper.

Now, let's hear from some of my beautiful friends.

"My name is Elizabeth Brown. I'm 15. I'm 5'10". I wear a medium in shirts. I'm caucasian. I have red hair and brown eyes. I play tennis and do theatre."

She is beautiful. She is valuable. She is worthy. She is accepted.

"My name is McKenley Coleman. I'm 15. I'm 5'7". I wear a size small in shirts. I'm caucasian. I have brown hair and green eyes. I'm involved in choir, drama, and writing."

She is beautiful. She is valuable. She is worthy. She is accepted.

"My name is Maddie Krumbach. I'm 14. I'm 5'3". I wear a size medium in shirts (but it fits a little big). I'm an Asian/white mix. I have brown hair and hazel eyes. I play basketball and track."

She is beautiful. She is valuable. She is worthy. She is accepted.

"My name is Kendal Minton. I'm 15. I'm 5'6". I wear a size small in shirts. I'm caucasian. I have blonde hair and green eyes. I wear glasses and contacts. I do cross country, track, and golf."

She is beautiful. She is valuable. She is worthy. She is accepted.

"My name is Maddie Herndon. I'm 5'3". I wear a medium or large in shirts. I'm caucasian. My hair is light brown but currently dyed blonde. I have hazel eyes. I wear glasses. I'm in FCCLA and play volleyball."

She is beautiful. She is valuable. She is worthy. She is accepted.

"My name is Lily Owens. I'm 15. I'm 5'10". I wear an X-Large in shirts. I'm caucasian. I have brown/blonde hair. I have blue/green eyes. I'm an actress and a singer."

She is beautiful. She is valuable. She is worthy. She is accepted.

"My name is Taylor Gann. I'm 12. I'm 5'1". I wear a small in shirts. I'm caucasian. I have brown hair that is currently highlighted with blonde streaks. I have hazel eyes. I'm a basketball player, equestrian, and singer."

She is beautiful. She is valuable. She is worthy. She is accepted.

"My name is Christeen Lee. I'm 15. I'm 5'9". I wear a large in shirts. I'm caucasian. I have blonde hair and blue/hazel eyes. I'm in FCCLA."

She is beautiful. She is valuable. She is worthy. She is accepted.

"My name is Quincey Martin. I'm 16. I'm 5'3". I wear a medium in shirts. I'm biracial. I have black hair and brown eyes. I cheer."

She is beautiful. She is valuable. She is worthy. She is accepted.

"My name is Maddie Teat. I'm 16. I'm 5'10". I wear a size large in shirts. I'm caucasian. I have blue eyes. I wear glasses and contacts. I do volleyball, soccer, FBLA, National Honor Society, and student council."

She is beautiful. She is valuable. She is worthy. She is accepted.

"My name is Lindsey Engler. I'm 14. I'm 5'5". I wear a size medium in shirts. I'm caucasian. I have brown hair and green eyes. I played basketball and softball."

She is beautiful. She is valuable. She is worthy. She is accepted.

"My name is Ava Wilson. I'm 15. I'm 5'4". I wear a size medium in shirts. I'm caucasian. I have brown hair and hazel eyes. I like to skateboard."

She is beautiful. She is valuable. She is worthy. She is accepted.

"My name is Autumn Courtney. I'm 18. I'm 5'7". I wear a size X-Large in shirts. I'm biracial. I have brown hair and brown eyes. I love traveling and hanging out with my friends."

She is beautiful. She is valuable. She is worthy. She is accepted.

Now insert your name, height, age, shirt size, race, ethnicity, hobbies, etc.

You are beautiful. You are valuable. You are worthy. You are accepted.

Look at that. All of these girls. All of these amazing qualities. All of these differences. We're still beautiful. Every single one of us. No one is higher on the scale. We're all in a straight line, and we're standing hand in hand, fighting against what society has defined as "beauty".

Dear society,

We are beautiful. We are valuable. We are worthy. We are loved. We are more precious than rubies. And guess what? We don't care what you have to say. We are perfect just the way we are.

The Author's Note

Wow. WOW! That was one heck of a journey.

I don't know how authors can spend a year on a book. This took me a month, and I'm worn out. That being said, I wouldn't trade this experience for the world.

All my life, I've never felt comfortable in my own skin. I looked different from the people I saw around me, and I always considered that a bad thing. I thought my beauty was lesser because they were beautiful too.

It took me years to get out of my funk. I carried myself as a confident person, but deep down, I wasn't. I used to want a nose job. I hated my glasses. None of my friends has them, and they wore contacts if they did. My hair couldn't seem to grow past my shoulders. I was often asked if I could change one thing, what would it be? I had trouble coming up with one answer.

Since then, I've been body shamed. I was introduced to body shaming fairly early, and I wasn't even insecure about what was made fun of. Soon after, I was. I fell into a pit. It took me a while to crawl out of it, but I did. My last resort was learning to accept who I am, and that's the best decision I've ever made.

Body shaming, insecurities, self-image issues, and even objectification are issues that every girl struggles with but is rarely talked about. This is dumb, but the kidz bop slogan is "By kids for kids". That's kind of what this book is: By a teenage girl who struggles with insecurities, for teenage girls who struggle with insecurities. I can relate to you. I understand you.

I've always had a way with words. Essays and writing assignments have always come easy to me. I've tried to write several books. I have all of these rough drafts with different fictional storylines and plots. I finished one in 6th grade, but we don't talk about that one (I cringed trying to read it the other day). Other than that, none of them have ever worked out for me. I've always been, well, stuck.

All of this started with an Instagram post, and then another one. Now, we're here.

Knowing that I've impacted so many girls is my favorite thing about this book. I didn't write this to get my name out there. I wrote this to show girls that society doesn't get to determine if you're beautiful or not. The LORD already established that; I'm just trying to help you believe it.

I would like to thank a few people. I know this isn't an "I just won an award speech", but there are a few people that need to be recognized.

The first one is McKenley Coleman. This girl has been my number one fan the entire time. She's helped me with ideas, formatting, and advice. This wouldn't have been possible without her. She's my only friend that writes, so she's been really helpful throughout this journey. She's reached out to me and asked how I'm doing. She's offered to help do whatever I need. She told me she's proud of me. She's hyped me up and helped me tremendously. I am truly blessed to have such an amazing woman by my side.

The second one is Maddie Krumbach. We used to play basketball together a long time ago, and we hadn't really talked since then. However, she's been such a great supporter. She's been encouraging, and overall a great friend. She's helped me make connections with other girls. She's reminded me several times that I'm an inspiration, which has helped me pursue this dream. Overall, she's the kindest soul, and I consider myself very lucky to call her a friend.

The third one is Lily Owens. Lily and I have been friends for years, but we have connected a lot more through this book. She told me about all the insecurities she struggled with, and we talked through it. Since then, she's been updating me on how she's feeling, and it's all positive news.

She's a constant reminder of why I decided to write this. She even bought her first bikini and wore it to the lake! How awesome is that? The answer: super awesome.

The last one is Faith Ireland. This one is very interesting. We actually weren't really friends before this started. We go to the same school, and we follow each other on Instagram, but that was about it. After I posted about confidence, she posted a selfie and tagged me in it with the caption: "Hey @reesemcca, thanks for the confidence boost." That's when I knew that the LORD was calling me to write this. She told me that she was really touched by what I had to say. I had no idea that my words were impacting people that much. So she pushed me into the direction of writing this.

Of course, I want to thank my family for supporting me throughout this journey. I'm only 15-years-old, so writing a book is kind of crazy. I'm overwhelmed with love and support, and I'm so grateful.

Lastly, I want y'all to know that I understand loving yourself is hard, especially with the influence we're surrounded by. However, I know it's possible, and self-love is a beautiful thing. I used to be a girl who found her value in what other people said about her. I used to be a girl who hated how she looked. I used to be a girl who envied what everyone else around her had. Now, I'm a girl who finds her value in what the LORD says. I'm a girl who loves how she looks. I'm a girl who recognizes that she is beautiful because she looks different, not despite the fact. I'm a girl who understands that beauty on the inside shines just as much as beauty on the outside. I'm a girl who supports other girls. I'm a girl who knows she's perfect, just the way she is. And, all I'm trying to do, is help you become that girl, too.

xoxo, Reese

Made in the USA
Coppell, TX
22 August 2020